AF599106

OCEAN LIFE

MARINE REPTILES & FISH

by
Claudia Martin

Minneapolis, Minnesota

Credits

Cover and title page, © LFPuntel/Getty Images; 3, © dstephens/iStock; 4–5, © Georgette Douwma/Getty Images; 4, © Dimitri Otis/Getty Images; 5, © SeaTops/Alamy Stock Photo; 6, © Anna Filippenok/Shutterstock, © Gena Melendrez/ Shutterstock, © Shane Gross/Shutterstock, and © Joe Quinn/Shutterstock; 7, © aquapix/Shutterstock and © Paulo Oliveira/ Alamy Stock Photo; 8–9, © Alex Rush/Shutterstock; 8, © Sergey Uryadnikov/Shutterstock and © Antonio Busiello/Robert Harding/Alamy Stock Photo; 9, © makeitahabit/Shutterstock; 10–11, © Reinhard Dirscherl/Alamy Stock Photo; 10, © Bruce Rasner, Jeffrey Rotman/Biosphoto/FLPA Images and © Andrea Izzotti/Shutterstock; 11, © Mark Willian Kirkland/ Shutterstock; 12–13, © Norbert Wu/Minden Pictures/FLPA Images; 12, © Andrea Izzotti/Shutterstock and © Laura Dinraths/Shutterstock; 13, © Roman Vintonyak/Shutterstock; 14–15, © WaterFrame/Alamy Stock Photo; 14, © Mark Conlin/ Alamy Stock Photo and © Helmut Corneli/Alamy Stock Photo; 15, © imageBROKER.com GmbH & Co. KG/Alamy Stock Photo and © Andriy Nekrasov/iStock; 16–17, © scubaluna/Shutterstock; 16, © Tropical studio/Shutterstock and © Steve Trewhella/FLPA Images; 17, © Arco Images GmbH/G. Lacz/Alamy Stock Photo; 18–19, © Norbert Probst/Imagebroker/ FLPA Images; 18, © Photo Researchers/FLPA Images and © Gerald Robert Fischer/Shutterstock; 19, © Michael Warwick/ Shutterstock; 20–21, © Michael Siluk/Alamy Stock Photo; 20, © Cigdem Sean Cooper/Shutterstock, © Cigdem Sean Cooper/Shutterstock, and © Alex_Vinci/Shutterstock; 21, © Dennis Jacobsen/Shutterstock; 22–23, © viridis/Getty Images; 22, © divedog/Shutterstock and © Silk-stocking/Shutterstock; 23, © ligio/Shutterstock; 24–25, © besjunior/Shutterstock; 24, © yaodiving/Shutterstock, © Kichigin/Shutterstock, and © NaniP/Shutterstock; 25, © orlandin/Shutterstock; 26–27, © marrio31/Getty Images; 26, © Anne Frijling/Shutterstock and © cbimages/Alamy Stock Photo; 27, © orlandin/ Shutterstock; 28–29, © Rodrigo Friscione/Getty Images; 28, © David Fleetham/Alamy Stock Photo and © WaterFrame/ Alamy Stock Photo; 29, © lunamarina/Shutterstock; 30–31, © Blue Planet Archive/Alamy Stock Photo; 30, © Mike Parry/ Minden Pictures/FLPA Images and © Tomas Kotouc/Shutterstock; 31, © Stephanie Rousseau/Shutterstock; 32–33, © Danita Delimont/Alamy Stock Photo; 32, © Maridav/Alamy Stock Photo, © Nature Picture Library/Alamy Stock Photo, and © mantaphoto/iStock; 33, © Dave Currey/Alamy Stock Photo; 34–35, © Georgette Douwma/Getty Images; 34, © shakeelmsm/Shutterstock and © SeaTops/Alamy Stock Photo; 35, © William Healy Photography/Shutterstock; 36–37, © Reinhard Dirscherl/Alamy Stock Photo; 36, © mauritius images GmbH/Alamy Stock Photo and © Ken Griffiths/iStock; 37, © RibeirodosSantos/iStock and © Magnus Lungren / Wild Wonders of China/Minden Pictures; 38–39, © WaterFrame/Alamy Stock Photo; 38, © Ery Azmeer/Shutterstock and © Elements_Brisbane/Shutterstock; 39, © ANDREY GUDKOV/Alamy Stock Photo; 40–41, © Daniel Heuclin/Biosphoto; 40, © cbstockfoto/Alamy Stock Photo and © Matthijs Kuijpers/Alamy Stock Photo; 41, © Sherry Epley/Alamy Stock Photo and © Howe Hoi/iStock; 42, © Humberto Ramirez/Getty Images; 43, © Terry Whittaker/Minden Pictures and © Gerard Soury/Getty Images; 47, © Gerald Corsi/iStock; 44–48, © dstephens/iStock.

Bearport Publishing Company Product Development Team

Publisher: Jen Jenson; Director of Product Development: Spencer Brinker; Managing Editor: Allison Juda; Editor: Cole Nelson; Associate Editor: Naomi Reich; Associate Editor: Tiana Tran; Art Director: Colin O'Dea; Designer: Kim Jones; Designer: Kayla Eggert; Product Development Specialist: Owen Hamlin

Statement on Usage of Generative Artificial Intelligence

Bearport Publishing remains committed to publishing high-quality nonfiction books. Therefore, we restrict the use of generative AI to ensure accuracy of all text and visual components pertaining to a book's subject. See BearportPublishing.com for details.

Library of Congress Cataloging-in-Publication Data is available at www.loc.gov or upon request from the publisher.

ISBN: 979-8-89232-893-7 (hardcover)
ISBN: 979-8-89232-923-1 (ebook)

For more information, write to Bearport Publishing, 5357 Penn Avenue South, Minneapolis, MN 55419.

Contents

Where It All Began

Life on Earth began in the ocean. About 3.5 billion years ago, it all started with single-celled microbes, but life soon became much more complex. The first fish developed around 500 million years ago. About 200 million years later, marine reptiles appeared as well. Now, the ocean teems with a wide variety of life. More than 20,000 species of fish and about 100 species of reptiles populate the ocean.

Life in the Ocean

Marine animals thrive in the ocean thanks to unique adaptations. Fish spend their lives underwater and breathe with gills. Marine reptiles do not have gills, so they must come to the surface to breathe air. Some reptiles have special glands that remove the salt from ocean water they take in.

The Food Web

The ocean's food web is complex. Small fish eat plants and tiny sea creatures. Sharks are apex predators that eat larger fish and marine reptiles, while rarely being hunted themselves. Larger fish and some marine reptiles hunt small fish. And creatures big and small that die in the water sink to the bottom, decay, and become nutrients for sea plants, continuing the food web.

Diving Deep

Scientists think they have discovered only about 10 percent of the species that live in the ocean. They are constantly on the hunt for more. In 2024, one expedition of researchers spent 3 weeks sending nets and cameras 3 miles (5 km) deep. While they may have found as many as 100 new species, many more are yet to be discovered.

Marine Fish

About 20,000 species of fish live in the ocean. Many have skin covered in hard plates called scales and breathe by taking oxygen from the water using their gills. Most fish swim through the wet environment by waving their body or tail while steering with their fins.

Breathing through Gills

Like most animals, fish need oxygen to live. There is oxygen in the ocean, but it is dissolved and spread out in the water. Fish get this oxygen by gulping water into their mouths. The water flows past and out of tiny slits in their sides called gills. These gills are filled with tiny blood vessels that soak up the oxygen and release the remaining water.

Classes of Fish

There are three classes of fish. Each class has different body features.

JAWLESS FISH

CHARACTERISTICS:
These fish have no jaws for biting, so they feed by sucking. Their bodies are long and scaleless.

SPECIES:
Hagfish and lampreys

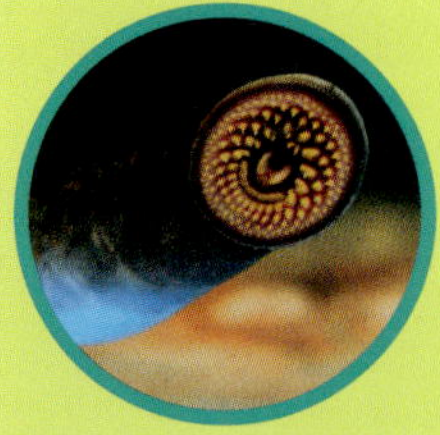

A lamprey mouth

CARTILAGINOUS FISH

CHARACTERISTICS:
This class has jaws and a skeleton made of bendy cartilage. The skin of creatures in this class has many toothlike scales.

SPECIES:
Sharks, skates, and rays

Thresher shark

BONY FISH

CHARACTERISTICS:
These jawed fish have skeletons made of bone. They are usually covered in smooth, overlapping scales.

SPECIES:
All other fish

Yellowtail snapper

DID YOU KNOW? Female sunfish produce more eggs than any other fish, releasing up to 300 million of them at a time.

Hunting Sharks

Sharks have skeletons made of bendy, lightweight cartilage rather than bone. Their mouths have several rows of teeth that are constantly moving forward, falling out, and then being replaced by new teeth. Most sharks are fierce predators, using their teeth for grabbing, biting, or crushing prey.

Shark Senses

Sharks have excellent smell, sight, and hearing. Like most fish, sharks also have a sense system called the lateral line, which uses hairlike cells that feel water movements to detect what is happening around them. In addition, sharks and other cartilaginous fish have sensing organs called ampullae of Lorenzini, which are jelly-filled pores in the skin. These detect the electric fields created by the moving muscles of other animals.

Growing up to 20 ft. (6.1m) long and reaching speeds of 35 mph (56 kph), the great white shark is a fearsome predator. This adult is swallowing a whole seal.

This Caribbean reef shark has closed its nictitating membrane while holding a struggling lionfish.

Eye Protection

Many sharks have an extra, see-through eyelid called a nictitating membrane. They close this membrane to protect their eyes when striking prey or being attacked. Some species, such as great white sharks, do not have a nictitating membrane, so they roll their eyeballs backward when lunging at prey.

SAND TIGER

Length: Up to 10.5 ft. (3.2 m)

Range: Subtropical and temperate Atlantic, Indian, and Pacific Oceans

Habitat: Coastal waters to depths of up to 620 ft. (190 m)

Diet: Bony fish, rays, skates, and smaller sharks

Conservation: Population shrinking due to fishing

The scalloped hammerhead shark has eyes at either side of its hammer-shaped head. This means the shark can see above, below, in front, and behind itself.

As with other sharks, the hammerhead's gill slits are not covered. The slits are where water exits the body, after oxygen has been taken from it.

This shark usually hunts fish, such as sardines and mackerel.

DID YOU KNOW? When chasing prey, the shortfin mako shark can swim up to 45 mph (72 kph) and leap up to 20 ft. (6 m) out of the water.

Filter Feeding Sharks

Three species of sharks use a method of feeding that is different from their fierce relatives. Whale, megamouth, and basking sharks are filter feeders. They eat tiny zooplankton and fish by straining them out of the water.

Whale shark skin, which is up to 4 in. (10 cm) thick, is dotted with pale spots.

Big Mouths

Filter feeding sharks have huge mouths. The largest of all is the whale shark's, which is 4.9 ft. (1.5 m) wide. Filter feeders have two feeding methods. Either they swim forward with their mouths wide open so that food-filled water rushes inside, or they suck in mouthfuls of water. As the water flows out of the back of the mouth through the gills, filter pads in the gills act like sieves, catching tiny animals in the water.

Whalesharks feed on small fish, squid, and zooplankton.

The megamouth shark is so rare that no one knew it existed until 1976. Reaching 17 ft. (5.1 m), it is the smallest of the filter feeding sharks.

WHALE SHARK

Length: Up to 40 ft. (12 m)

Range: Tropical and subtropical Atlantic, Indian, and Pacific Oceans

Habitat: Open ocean to depths of 6,300 ft. (1,920 m)

Diet: Zooplankton, small fish, and squid

Conservation: Endangered due to fishing and collisions with boats

DID YOU KNOW? The whale shark is not just the largest fish but the largest animal that is not a mammal.

Threatened Sharks

Of the more than 500 species of sharks, more than 100 are endangered, including whale and basking sharks. Every year, as many as 100 million sharks are killed by fishermen. Most sharks give birth to a small number of young. As a result, some shark species cannot reproduce fast enough to keep up their numbers.

Rays and Relatives

The giant oceanic manta ray can grow up to 29 ft. (8.8 m) wide.

Rays—including skates, guitarfish, and sawfish—make up a group of fish called batoids. Like sharks, batoids have skeletons made of cartilage. They are flat bodied, and many species have extra-large, often winglike pectoral fins.

Flapping or Waving

Most batoids swim by moving their pectoral fins. This makes them different from sharks and most other fish, which power through the water using movements in their tails or bodies. Batoids such as manta rays and eagle rays have wide, pointed pectoral fins that they flap up and down, almost like birds. Batoids with rounder pectoral fins, such as electric rays, wave their fins with a ruffling wave that travels along the length of each fin.

The largest spotted eagle rays grow up to 16 ft. (4.9 m) long, with a wingspan of up to 10 ft. (3 m).

Electric Rays

The 69 species of electric rays make electricity in special organs on either side of their heads. All living things, including humans, make tiny amounts of electricity as their bodies work, but electric rays make larger amounts and then store it like energy in a battery. These rays can release a pulse of electricity to kill or stun prey. It can also be used for defense.

The leopard torpedo ray is a species of electric ray that uses electricity to stun fish, worms, and crustaceans.

DID YOU KNOW? The largest species of electric rays make deadly electric pulses of up to 220 volts.

BROWN GUITARFISH

Length: Up to 40 in. (100 cm)

Range: Tropical and subtropical coasts of the western Pacific Ocean

Habitat: Sandy and muddy seabeds to depths of up to 750 ft. (230 m)

Diet: Fish, shrimp, and squid

Conservation: Not known

Eels

Eels are bony fish with long, snakelike bodies. Although most live in salt water, some spend their adult lives in fresh water. Eels spend their days hidden in mud, sand, or holes in rocks and coral reefs. At night, they come out to hunt.

Eels hunt using their excellent sense of smell rather than by sight.

Mysteries of the Ocean

Eels change a lot as they grow up. For hundreds of years, scientists didn't know how eels were born. They even thought eel larvae and adults were different species. Now, scientists know that eels hatch as tiny, see-through larvae. They grow into larger glass eels. Most glass eels travel up rivers to live in fresh water. Eventually, they grow into silver eels and travel all the way back to the ocean to mate.

American eels live in fresh water but migrate thousands of miles to lay their eggs in the ocean.

Ambush Hunting

Eels are carnivores that eat whatever they can catch, including insects, fish, shrimp, crabs, and clams. Some species even eat other eels. Eels hunt at night, and many are ambush predators. They hide in rocks and coral reefs before lunging out, using their strong jaws and sharp teeth to snatch prey.

Spotted garden eels live in colonies on the seafloor. They feed on tiny animals called zooplankton.

DID YOU KNOW? There are 800 species of eels, but electric eels aren't included. Electric eels are more closely related to carp and catfish.

Slender giant moray eels are the longest eels in the world, growing up to 13 ft. (4 m) long.
Eels cover their bodies in a mucus that protects their smooth skin.
Eels are predatory fish with strong jaws and sharp teeth.
EEL RECORDS
Length: Up to 156 in. (396 cm)
Weight: Up to 240 lb. (109 kg)
Lifespan: Up to 20 years
Habitat: Fresh water and salt water
Conservation: Some species critically endangered

Flatfish

Like most fish, flatfish have skeletons made of bone. They live on the seafloor throughout the ocean, from the Arctic to the shores of Antarctica. With their flattened bodies, they are able to lie on their sides as they wait motionless for passing prey.

The wide-eyed flounder has both eyes on its left side. Like other flatfish, it can stick up its eyes to get a better view.

Camouflage

Many flatfish are well camouflaged on the seafloor. Although their undersides are pale, their tops are usually dappled or spotted to match the seabed. Some flatfish, such as flounder, can change their skin color by releasing pigments to make their spots darker, lighter, bigger, or smaller.

This sole is burying itself in sand for extra camouflage.

Moving Eyes

Flatfish are symmetrical when they hatch from their eggs, with one eye on each side of their bodies. At this stage, they drift through the water rather than living on the bottom. As flatfish grow into adults, one of their eyes moves to the other side of their heads. Then, the fish sink to the bottom, laying their eyeless sides on the floor.

The European plaice lies with its eyed side facing up.

TURBOT

Length: Up to 40 in. (100 cm)

Range: European coasts of the northern Atlantic Ocean

Habitat: Sandy or rocky seabeds at depths of up to 460 ft. (140 m)

Diet: Fish, crustaceans, and bivalves

Conservation: Population shrinking

This flounder is waiting to ambush fish and shrimp.

A flatfish's dorsal fin extends around the head. Flatfish belong to the subclass of ray-finned fish, so their fins are supported by bony spines called rays.

DID YOU KNOW? Peacock flounders can change their color to suit their surroundings in 8 seconds.

Seahorses

Seahorses are small fish that are covered not in scales but in bony plates of armor. This makes them unable to wiggle their bodies to swim, so they flutter their fins to move along slowly. Seahorses are such poor swimmers that they usually remain still, using their curling tails to grip seaweed or coral to keep them in place.

Fathers Giving Birth

Seahorses have a unique method of giving birth. Before mating, a male and female seahorse court each other, dancing snout to snout and holding tails. When she is ready, the female seahorse puts anywhere from 50 to 1,500 eggs into a pouch on the male's front. The male carries the eggs until they hatch. Then, he releases the tiny young, called fry, into the water.

This male dwarf seahorse is releasing his fry into the water.

A seahorse sucks up microorganisms and tiny crustaceans through its toothless snout.

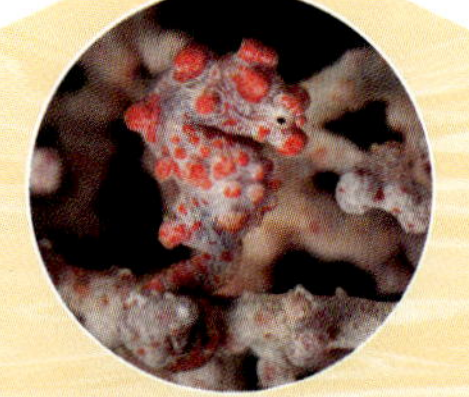

BARGIBANT'S PYGMY SEAHORSE

Length: Up to 1 in. (2.4 cm)

Range: Tropical coasts of the eastern Indian and western Pacific Oceans

Habitat: Sea fan corals at depths of up to 130 ft. (40 m)

Diet: Tiny crustaceans

Conservation: Small population that may need future protection

Sea Dragons

The three species of sea dragons belong to the same family as seahorses. They also have body armor and long snouts for sucking up food. Unlike seahorses, which are among the few fish to swim upright, sea dragons swim horizontally and do not have curling tails. Male sea dragons also take care of their eggs, but they carry them on their tails rather than in a pouch.

DID YOU KNOW? The world's slowest-moving fish is the dwarf seahorse, which has a top speed of only 5 ft. (1.5 m) per hour.

Boxfish and Relatives

The horned boxfish, also called the longhorn cowfish, lives in coral reefs.

Boxfish, sunfish, porcupinefish, pufferfish, and triggerfish all belong to an order of bony fish called Tetraodontiformes, meaning four teeth in ancient Greek. Their unusual jaws form beak shapes with toothlike bones that are often used for crushing hard-shelled invertebrates.

Strange Bodies

Most fish in this order are covered in bony plates, sharp spines, or tough skin. Their bodies are rigid, so they do not wriggle to swim. Instead, they move by waving their fins. These fish are also known for their strange body shapes, which may be nearly square (boxfish), round (porcupinefish), or flattened (sunfish and triggerfish).

A sunfish's body ends behind the dorsal and anal fins, making the fish look as if it has lost its back half.

Puffing Up

Porcupinefish and pufferfish have a very effective defense when they are threatened by predators. They fill their stretchy stomachs with water, which allows them to puff up until they are too big for most predators to swallow. In addition, they are covered by sharp spines, and many pufferfish are extremely poisonous.

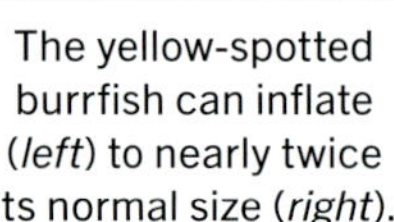

The yellow-spotted burrfish can inflate (*left*) to nearly twice its normal size (*right*).

CLOWN TRIGGERFISH

Length: Up to 20 in. (50 cm)

Range: Tropical and subtropical coasts of the Indian and Pacific Oceans

Habitat: Coral reefs to depths of up to 250 ft. (76 m)

Diet: Mollusks, crustaceans, and sea urchins

Conservation: Not known

These tough horns may make this fish harder to swallow. When threatened, the boxfish also releases poisonous mucus through its skin.

This boxfish eats algae, worms, crustaceans, and mollusks.

DID YOU KNOW? The bumphead sunfish is the heaviest bony fish, weighing up to 6,050 lb. (2,740 kg).

Surgeonfish and Relatives

Surgeonfish, tangs, and unicornfish usually live on coral reefs. On either side of their bodies, at the base of their tails, these fish have sharp spines, much like a surgeon's knife. While some species have fixed spines, others have hinged spines that can be flicked out with a twist of the tail.

Safety in Numbers

Fish in this family feed on algae that grows on coral reefs, grazing on it with their sharp teeth. Patches of algae are often guarded by aggressive damselfish. So, surgeonfish and their relatives often feed in groups, which offers them defense against damselfish and other predators.

These powder blue tangs are swimming in groups called shoals for safety. When the fish are all swimming in the same direction, it is called schooling.

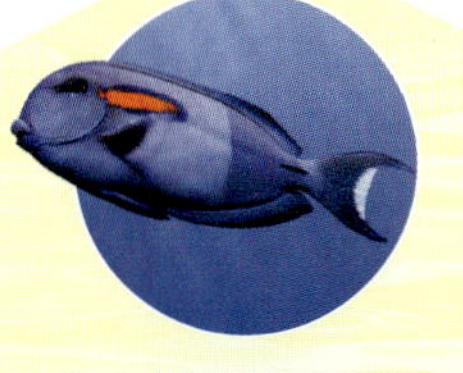

ORANGESPOT SURGEONFISH

Length: Up to 14 in. (35 cm)

Range: Tropical coasts of the eastern Indian and western Pacific Oceans

Habitat: Coral reefs to depths of up to 270 ft. (80 m)

Diet: Algae and diatoms

Conservation: Not at risk

Unicornfish

As most unicornfish reach adulthood, they grow bony, hornlike spikes between their eyes. Males grow bigger horns than females. Scientists are not sure what the horns do, since the fish do not use them for fighting. It is likely that the growth signals that fish are old enough for mating.

DID YOU KNOW? The spines of the lined surgeonfish are venomous. They can give humans painful wounds and kill smaller predators.

Scorpionfish

Many of the world's most venomous species of fish are scorpionfish. These fish inject predators with venom through a prick with one of their sharp spines, which contain venom-making glands. Most species of scorpionfish live on or near the seafloor in the ocean's warmer regions.

The 13 long spines of the dorsal fin contain venom glands. There is also a venomous spine in each of the 2 pelvic fins and 3 in the anal fin, making 18 in total.

Sucking Up

Scorpionfish capture prey through suction feeding. Some scorpionfish lie in wait for prey while others actively hunt. But when prey gets close, they all behave the same way. In a fraction of a second, the scorpionfish opens its mouth and expands its cheeks. Water and any prey are sucked into the scorpionfish's mouth to fill the space.

Reef Stonefish

The most venomous fish of all is the reef stonefish. This creature lives in the coral reefs of the tropical Indian and Pacific Oceans. A prick from the stonefish's spines can be deadly to humans. This fish is especially dangerous to humans because it blends in on the seafloor, looking just like a rock, as it waits for prey to ambush.

This camouflaged tasselled scorpionfish lies in wait for passing fish and crustaceans.

This reef stonefish is camouflaged to look like an algae-covered rock (*left*). It can bury itself in sand to become even less visible (*right*).

SHORTFIN DWARF LIONFISH

Length: Up to 7 in. (18 cm)

Range: Tropical coasts of the Indian and western Pacific Oceans

Habitat: Coral reefs to depths of up to 260 ft. (80 m)

Diet: Small crustaceans

Conservation: Not at risk

A member of the scorpionfish family, the common lionfish hunts small fish and crustaceans.

The fanlike pectoral fins are not venomous.

DID YOU KNOW? Like some animals on land, lionfish have bold patterns to warn predators that they are dangerous to eat.

Dragonets

These small fish live mainly in the tropical waters of the Indian and Pacific Oceans. Dragonets are usually colorful and highly patterned, with large fins. These flashy features can be useful as camouflage or as a way of attracting a mate. Dragonets stay close to sandy seafloors, where they bury themselves to escape predators.

Courting

Before mating, male and female dragonets court each other. During courtship, the two fish spread and display their fins. Then, the pair swims upward side by side, rubbing against each other. When they get near the surface, the female releases her eggs and the male releases his sperm into the water. The fertilized eggs float away.

Like all dragonets, male and female mandarin dragonets look different from one another. The males (*left*) are bigger, have longer fins, and are differently patterned.

Fighting

Male dragonets are very aggressive toward one another. They most often fight over females, but sometimes they just fight to show their strength. During fights, the males chase, wrestle, and bite. Fights often end with the death of the weaker male.

These two male butterfly dragonets are battling head to head. This species lives only around the coasts of Australia.

STARRY DRAGONET

Length: Up to 3 in. (7.5 cm)
Range: Tropical coasts of the Indian Ocean
Habitat: Coral reefs at depths of up to 75 ft. (23 m)
Diet: Small crustaceans, worms, and microorganisms
Conservation: Not at risk

Dragonets have large eyes positioned on the tops of their heads. When the dragonet buries itself in sand for defense, its eyes stay uncovered to keep watch.

The picturesque dragonet's bright patterns help with camouflage in its colorful coral reef habitat.

Dragonets protect their skin with a coating of thick, slimy mucus.

DID YOU KNOW? The mandarin dragonet got its name from its colorful pattern, which is like the robes worn by mandarin officials who worked for the emperor of China.

Billfish

These large bony fish are fierce predators. They have long bills, or beaks, which are extensions of their upper jaw bones. The bills are used for slashing at prey—and occasionally for spearing it. Billfish include sailfish, marlins, and swordfish.

Fastest Fish

Billfish usually live in the open ocean, far from land. Their long, streamlined bodies and powerful muscles make them excellent swimmers. They travel vast distances in search of food. When pursuing prey, billfish are the fastest fish in the ocean. Scientists do not agree which billfish is the fastest. Some say it is the Indo-Pacific sailfish, while others name the black marlin as the quickest fish in the sea.

The Atlantic sailfish has a large, sail-like dorsal fin that it folds down while swimming. When attacking prey, it raises the sail to steady its side-to-side movements.

The black marlin has been recorded at speeds of up to 80 mph (128 kph).

Swordfish

The swordfish has the longest bill of all billfish, reaching 5 ft. (1.5 m). While the bills of other billfish are rounder and more spearlike, the swordfish's is sword-shaped. It is flat, smooth, and sharp. Although some billfish have been known to spear prey and predators, swordfish use their bills only for slashing.

The swordfish hunts alone, chasing smaller fish, such as mackerel and herring, as well as descending to find crustaceans and squid in the darker waters below.

DID YOU KNOW? The biggest billfish is the Indo-Pacific blue marlin, which can grow up to 16.4 ft. (5 m) long.

WHITE MARLIN

Length: Up to 9.2 ft. (2.8 m)

Range: Tropical and subtropical Atlantic Ocean

Habitat: Open ocean to depths of 980 ft. (300 m)

Diet: Fish, such as flying fish and tuna, as well as squid

Conservation: Population at risk from sport fishing and accidental capture in nets

Marine Reptiles

The first reptiles lived on land, but around 250 million years ago, some reptiles adapted to life in the ocean. Today, there are around 10,000 species of reptiles on Earth, but only about 100 are marine. Reptiles need to breathe air, so marine reptiles need to come to the surface regularly.

Groups of Marine Reptiles

Marine reptiles belong to three orders. The turtle order contains seven species of sea turtles. The crocodilian order contains two species of crocodiles that swim in the ocean. The squamate order has a single species of marine iguanas and about 70 species of sea snakes. Squamates have skin protected by small, overlapping scales while turtles and crocodiles grow harder bony plates called scutes.

To break out of its tough shell, a baby saltwater crocodile uses a horny piece of skin on the tip of its snout called an egg-tooth.

The yellow-lipped sea krait kills eels and other fish by injecting a dose of killer venom using sharp fangs.

Sea Snakes

Of all marine reptiles, sea snakes are best adapted to life in the ocean. While most marine reptiles have to go ashore to lay eggs and rest, the majority of sea snakes never leave the ocean. Most give birth to live young in the water. Only the sea snakes known as kraits go on land to lay eggs.

Although it must surface eventually to breathe, a sea snake can absorb some oxygen from the water through its skin.

DID YOU KNOW? The sea snake with the deadliest venom is the Dubois' sea snake, but luckily it has small fangs and is not very aggressive.

MARINE REPTILE RECORDS

Heaviest: Saltwater crocodile, up to 2,650 lb. (1,200 kg)

Longest turtle: Leatherback sea turtle, up to 7 ft. (2.1 m) long

Shortest: Marine iguana, as small as 11 in. (28 cm) long

Fastest swimmer: Leatherback sea turtle, up to 22 mph (35 kph)

Longest living: Saltwater crocodile, possibly more than 100 years

Marine Iguanas

Marine iguanas are the only lizards that find their food in the sea. They live on the Galápagos Islands, a chain of volcanic islands about 600 miles (970 km) off Ecuador's coast. These iguanas differ slightly in size, color, and shape from island to island.

Iguana Life Cycle

During mating season, male marine iguanas compete by pushing their heads together until the weaker one gives up. Females dig burrows in sand or volcanic ash and lay up to six eggs, then guard the nest for several days. Young marine iguanas hatch about 95 days later.

Male marine iguanas may become brighter and even change colors during mating season.

Foraging in the Sea

Marine iguanas forage for algae in the sea. Small marine iguanas hunt for algae close to the shore during low tide. Larger ones swim out during high tide and may dive down 65 ft. (20 m). They can stay underwater for up to 30 minutes at a time.

A marine iguana swims by wiggling its body like a snake.

MARINE IGUANA

Length: Up to 5 ft. (1.5 m)
Weight: Up to 3.3 lb. (1.5 kg)
Lifespan: Up to 12 years
Habitat: Beaches and rocky shores of the Galápagos Islands
Conservation: Vulnerable

DID YOU KNOW? A special gland in the marine iguana's head removes salt from its body. Then, it sneezes out the extra salt.

Sea Turtles

There are seven species of sea turtles. From smallest to largest, they are the Kemp's ridley, olive ridley, hawksbill, flatback, green, loggerhead, and leatherback. A sea turtle's large but streamlined body is protected by a shell divided into two parts. The animal's back is covered by a carapace, while their underside is covered by a plastron.

Nesting on a Beach

At the start of mating season, sea turtles swim from their feeding grounds to their coastal mating areas—places that may be thousands of miles apart. When a female is ready to lay her eggs, she climbs onto the beach, usually at night, and digs a hole in the sand using her back flippers. She lays a clutch of soft-shelled eggs, covers them with sand to hide them, and then returns to the sea. After 50 to 60 days, the babies hatch. Females are born from eggs that stayed warmer while males hatch from cooler eggs.

Loggerhead turtles always make their nests on the beaches where they were born. They make about 4 nests per season and lay around 100 eggs in each nest.

This olive ridley turtle is swimming through plastic trash.

At Risk

Sea turtles are among the world's most threatened animals. The green turtle is endangered, and the Kemp's ridley and hawksbill turtles are critically endangered. These turtles are put at risk by damage to their nesting beaches, pollution in the water, fishing nets that easily tangle turtles, and rising sea temperatures.

FLATBACK TURTLE

Length: Up to 48 in. (122 cm)

Range: Coastal waters of Australia and New Guinea, in the Indian and Pacific Oceans

Habitat: Tropical and subtropical waters with soft seabeds, at depths of up to 200 ft. (60 m)

Diet: Soft coral, shrimp, jellyfish, and sea cucumbers

Conservation: At risk from habitat damage and pollution

The hawksbill sea turtle's mouth is sharp and hooked like a beak, which makes it ideal for eating tough sea sponges, algae, and jellyfish.

This turtle's carapace is made up of 13 overlapping bony plates called scutes.

Growing to around 45 in. (114 cm) long, the hawksbill lives mainly on tropical coral reefs in the Atlantic, Indian, and Pacific Oceans.

DID YOU KNOW? The green turtle can survive for more than 80 years in the wild. It is the longest-living turtle species.

Sea Snakes

Some of the world's most venomous snakes live in salt water. About 70 species of sea snakes can be found in the tropical waters of the Pacific and Indian Oceans. Sea snakes spend their lives in the water, but they must come up to the surface to breathe air.

Life Cycle

Sea snakes rarely leave the water, even when it comes time to have young. After mating, females carry eggs inside their bodies until they hatch. Then, the mothers give birth to live young in the ocean. Mother sea snakes usually have up to 9 babies at a time, but some have had as many as 34!

Male olive sea snakes sometimes swim at divers, mistaking them for other olive sea snakes.

Lying in Wait

Sea snakes hunt along reefs, in seagrass meadows, and on the seafloor. While hunting, they stay underwater for long stretches of time, sometimes holding their breath for several hours. Then, when it's time to strike, they lunge at passing fish, inject deadly venom with their short fangs, and swallow their meal whole.

YELLOW-BELLIED SEA SNAKE

Length: Up to 8.9 ft. (2.7 m)

Weight: Up to 2.9 lb. (1.3 kg)

Lifespan: Up to 10 years

Range: Shallow, tropical waters of the eastern Pacific and Indian Oceans

Conservation: Some species threatened by habitat loss due to climate change

DID YOU KNOW? Yellow-bellied sea snakes may dive as deep as 50 ft. (15 m) to hunt.

Crocodiles

Only a few species of crocodiles swim in the oceans. Like most reptiles, they are cold-blooded, which means their bodies becomes hotter or colder depending on the temperature of the conditions around them. Crocodiles warm up after swimming by going ashore to bask in the sun.

American crocodiles look a lot like American alligators, but unlike alligators, their snouts taper in a triangle shape.

The Saltwater Crocodile

The saltwater crocodile lives along the coasts of northern Australia and southern Asia. As the largest living reptile with jaws up to 39 in. (100 cm) long, this crocodile is an apex predator. Its aggression makes it a threat to humans as well as its usual prey, which ranges from sharks to birds and crabs. This predator's method of hunting is very effective. It lies in wait, then swims at prey at up to 18 mph (29 kph). It either drowns its victim by pulling the creature underwater or swallows it whole.

The saltwater crocodile has one of the strongest bites of any animal.

AMERICAN CROCODILE

Length: Up to 20 ft. (6 m)

Range: Coasts of the Americas, from Florida to Peru, in the Atlantic and Pacific Oceans

Habitat: Ocean coasts, rivers, and swamps

Diet: Fish, frogs, turtles, birds, and small mammals

Conservation: Threatened by habitat loss

Cuban Crocodiles

Cuban crocodiles live in brackish water, meaning water that is partly fresh water and partly salt water. While they can be found in coastal swamps and marshes throughout Cuba, these crocodiles are also comfortable on land. They can run as fast as 22 mph (35 kph). Cuban crocodiles use their strong tails to push themselves out of the water in a leap to catch birds and other prey from trees hanging over the water.

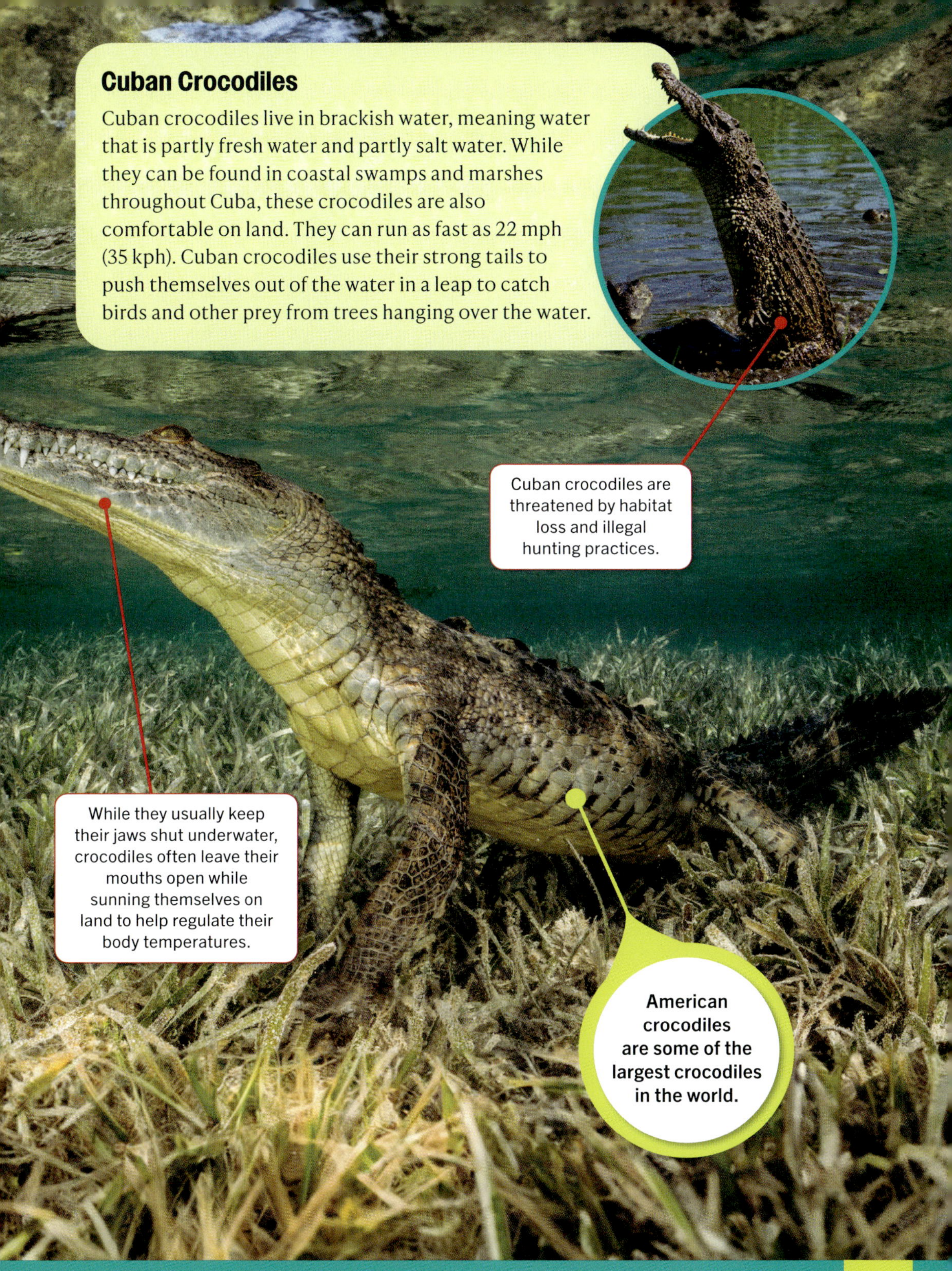

DID YOU KNOW? Saltwater crocodiles have 66 teeth, some of which reach up to 5 in. (13 cm) long.

Mangrove Monitors

A mangrove monitor finds prey with its keen eyesight.

Mangrove monitors are tropical reptiles that live in mangrove swamps, coastal forests, and rivers on the western Pacific Islands and in northern Australia. They are strong swimmers and good climbers. They can be found hunting in the water, basking on sunny rocks, or burrowing into the ground to hibernate for winter.

Mangrove monitors flick out their tongues to detect their prey's scent.

A Varied Diet

Mangrove monitors are carnivores that eat almost anything they can find. They chow down on fish, crabs, frogs, insects, birds, and other lizards. Their jaws can even unhinge and stretch to eat larger prey. Mangrove monitors hunt on land, in trees, and in the sea.

Mangrove monitors are territorial. Males sometimes fight over females.

Life Cycle

A female monitor may dig her burrow in sand or find a hollow log where she lays 2 to 12 eggs. The young hatch seven to eight months later, and they are immediately ready to hunt and live on their own.

DID YOU KNOW? Monitor lizards have glands that are very similar to snake venom glands. But scientists do not know yet if monitor lizards can create venom.

MANGROVE MONITOR

Length: Up to 6.6 ft. (2 m)
Weight: Up to 4.2 lb. (1.9 kg)
Lifespan: Up to 15 years
Range: Western Pacific, from Micronesia to northern Australia
Conservation: Not endangered

Marine Reptiles and Fish at Risk

Marine reptiles and fish have evolved to survive in complex ocean ecosystems. But recent human activities have made life harder for these animals. Pollution damages important coastal environments that are home to many species. Higher levels of greenhouse gases in the atmosphere and increasing ocean temperatures are bleaching and killing coral reefs that house thousands of species of fish. Some of these animals have become endangered or threatened. They need to be protected, or they risk becoming extinct.

Learning More

To help endangered fish and reptiles, some researchers attach tracking tags to the animals. They use satellites and research ships to gather data on the animals' health and movements. Underwater robots help scientists monitor known species and discover new ones. With data from these new technologies, scientists will learn more about how fish and reptile ecosystems work and how to protect them.

Scientists use remote-controlled robots to explore parts of the ocean too dangerous for humans to visit.

Reef Sharks

A 2023 study found the populations of 5 species of sharks that live around coral reefs have dropped an average of 63 percent. Two of the species, the gray reef shark and the Caribbean reef shark, are now considered endangered. Scientists say shark fishing caused the drop and recommended countries ban or limit shark fishing to protect these important ocean animals.

Review and Reflect

Now that you've read about marine reptiles and fish, let's review what you've learned. Use the following questions to reflect on your newfound knowledge and integrate it with what you already knew.

Check for Understanding

1. Describe how fish breathe underwater. *(See p. 6)*
2. What are some of the body parts sharks use to find and catch prey while hunting? *(See pp. 8–9)*
3. How big is the whale shark's mouth? Why does it need to be so large? *(See p. 10)*
4. In what ways are batoids different from most other fish in the ocean? *(See p. 12)*
5. What are the usual stages in the life cycle of an eel, and what are the names for eels in each? *(See p. 14)*
6. How do flatfish adapt to be able to see when they lie flat on the ocean floor? *(See p. 16)*
7. Describe how seahorses give birth. *(See p. 18)*
8. How do porcupinefish and pufferfish protect themselves? *(See p. 20)*
9. Why do some fish form groups to eat? *(See p. 22)*
10. What is the most venomous kind of fish? *(See p. 24)*
11. Name some of the reasons dragonets are colorful. *(See pp. 26–27)*
12. What are the different orders of marine reptiles? Name one reptile that belongs to each order. *(See p. 30)*
13. List some of the ways marine iguanas have evolved to adapt to their coastal environments. *(See pp. 32–33)*
14. What kind of water do Cuban crocodiles live in? *(See p. 39)*
15. How do mangrove monitors find their prey? *(See pp. 40–41)*

Making Connections

1. In what ways are sea dragons different from seahorses? In what ways are they similar?

2. How are sea snakes better adapted to live in the water than snakes found on land?

3. Some fish don't have scales. What are the ways these fish protect themselves?

4. How does being cold-blooded affect a marine reptile's behaviors?

5. Many of the fish in this book are venomous. Name some of them and describe why being venomous is a good or bad thing when living in the ocean.

In Your Own Words

1. Some marine reptiles lay their eggs on land. Others give birth in the ocean. What might be some advantages and disadvantages of either method?

2. Fish come in all sorts of different colors. What are some ways these colors help or hurt these fish?

3. Choose one of the fish in this book that interests you the most. How has it adapted to its environment? If you could give this fish different features, what would they be and how would those features help the fish?

4. Scientists are still exploring the ocean and discovering new things all the time. Imagine discovering a completely new animal. What features would a new marine species likely have to have stayed undiscovered for so long?

5. Many marine reptiles and fish are at risk of becoming endangered. Why is this a problem? What ideas do you have to help save animals at risk?

Glossary

algae simple plantlike living things that are usually found in and around water

bivalve a soft-bodied invertebrate that lives in a hinged two-part shell, such as a clam or mussel

blood vessel a tube that carries blood through an animal's body

camouflage the way the color and shape of an animal make it less visible in its habitat

cartilaginous with a skeleton made of bendy cartilage rather than bone

class a scientific group that includes animals with the same body plan, such as birds or bony fish

crustacean an arthropod with two pairs of antennae on its head, such as a crab

dorsal fin a fin on the back of a fish or a cetacean

endangered at risk of becoming extinct in the near future

evolve to change gradually over time

filter feeding straining food from the water using comb- or net-like body parts

fresh water unsalted water, such as that found in rivers, lakes, and ponds

gills organs in fish that take oxygen from water

gland a body part that makes a substance for use in the body or for release

habitat the natural home of a living thing

invertebrate an animal without a backbone, such as a crab, squid, or insect

larva a young stage in the life cycle of some invertebrates

mammal an animal that grows hair at some point in its life and feeds its young milk from its body

mollusk an invertebrate with a soft body and sometimes a hard shell, such as a slug, snail, clam, or octopus

predator an animal that hunts and eats other animals

prey an animal that is hunted by another animal for food

species groups of living things that look similar and can mate together

zooplankton tiny animals, eggs, and larvae that drift through the water

Read More

Gish, Melissa. *Rays (Living Wild).* Mankato, MN: Creative Education, 2024.

de la Bédoyère, Camilla. *Shark Habitats (In Focus Sharks).* Minneapolis: Lerner Publishing, 2020.

Hale, K. A. *Essential Reptiles (Essential Animals).* Minneapolis: ABDO Publishing, 2022.

Hein, Till. *The Curious World of Seahorses: The Life and Lore of a Marine Marvel.* Berkeley, CA: Graystone Books, 2023.

Learn More Online

1. Go to **FactSurfer.com** or scan the QR code below.
2. Enter "**Marine Reptiles & Fish**" into the search box.
3. Click on the cover of this book to see a list of websites.

Index